ROME
THE CITY AT A

CW00816133

Tridente
Green and largely ped
is full of treasures for t
such as the Museo dell'
Lungotevere in Augusta

Villa Borghese
The city's magnificent 17th-century park
is still a pleasure garden. Here you'll find
Romans of all ages strutting their stuff.

Il Palazzetto
This hotel is perfectly positioned, with rooms
overlooking the Spanish Steps, and is the best
choice for romantics or those with a passion
for Italian viniculture (Rome's International
Wine Academy is based here).
See p021

Trevi Fountain
The baroque wonder is the scene of cinema's
most famous late-night dip. It's touristy but
remains a must-see while you're in town.
Piazza di Trevi

Pantheon
Hadrian's 2nd-century, largely concrete
temple dedicated to the Roman gods is also
home to the tombs of Raphael and Vittorio
Emanuele II, the first king of a united Italy.
See p010

Scuderie del Quirinale
Housed in the former stables next to the
Palazzo del Quirinale, this major exhibition
space was renovated by Italian architect
Gae Aulenti. Stop off in the café or bookshop,
before taking a stroll around the piazza.
Piazza del Quirinale, T 06 3996 7700

INTRODUCTION
THE CHANGING FACE OF THE URBAN SCENE

After a pre-millennial spruce-up, Rome has become cleaner and more functional than ever before. Thanks to mammoth public investment and a new masterplan, the city has entered an era of architectural evolution on a scale not seen since Mussolini's monomaniacal frenzy. Obsolete industrial buildings in depressed areas are being reclaimed to celebrate the future instead of simply preserving the past, and areas just outside the city walls are going through a regeneration process, with art galleries, restaurants and multifunctional *centri sociali* (cultural spaces) springing up. Typically, Rome's bars and clubs are not subject to the swift turnaround of those in other metropolises, but a surge of openings in the past year has refreshed the urban life of the Eternal City.

Although Rome's Renaissance geniuses – Michelangelo, Bernini, Borromini – are hard acts to follow, contemporary architects have made their mark. Renzo Piano's Auditorium Parco della Musica (see po70) gave the city perfect acoustics; Richard Meier's 2006 museum, housing the Ara Pacis (see po1), doubles as an art space, whereas his Jubilee church (Via Francesco Tovaglieri) in Tor Tre Teste has become a destination for lovers of sacred architecture, as has Piero Sartogo and Nathalie Grenon's Chiesa del Santo Volto di Gesù in Magliana. Dutch architect Rem Koolhaas will be joining the list; his renovation of the former fruit and vegetable market in up-and-coming Ostiense is due to be finished by 2012.

ESSENTIAL INFO
FACTS, FIGURES AND USEFUL ADDRESSES

TOURIST OFFICE
Via Giovanni Giolitti 34
T 06 06 08
www.060608.it

TRANSPORT
Car hire
Hertz
T 06 474 0389
Public transport
T 06 57 003
www.metroroma.it
Last trains depart at 11.30pm; Sat, 12.30am
Taxis
La Capitale Radio Taxi
T 06 3570
Samarcanda
T 06 5551
There are also taxi ranks at main
squares and stations

EMERGENCY SERVICES
Ambulance
T 118
Fire
T 115
Police
T 113
24-hour pharmacy
Farmacia Notturna Internazionale
Piazza Barberini 49
T 06 482 5456

EMBASSIES
British Embassy
Via XX Settembre 80a
T 06 4220 0001
www.britain.it
US Embassy
Via Vittorio Veneto 119a
T 06 46 741
www.usembassy.it

MONEY
American Express
Piazza di Spagna 38
T 06 67 641
www.travel.americanexpress.com

POSTAL SERVICES
Post office
Piazza di San Silvestro 19
T 06 6973 7232
Shipping
UPS
T 800 877 877

BOOKS
The Films of Federico Fellini by Peter
Bondanella (Cambridge University Press)
Vitruvius: Ten Books on Architecture
(Cambridge University Press)
The Woman of Rome by Alberto Moravia
(Steerforth Press)

WEBSITES
Architecture/Design
www.maxxi.darc.beniculturali.it
Art
www.macro.roma.museum
Newspaper
www.repubblica.it

COST OF LIVING
**Taxi from Leonardo da Vinci Airport
to city centre**
€40
Cappuccino
€1
Packet of cigarettes
€4
Daily newspaper
€1
Bottle of champagne
€70

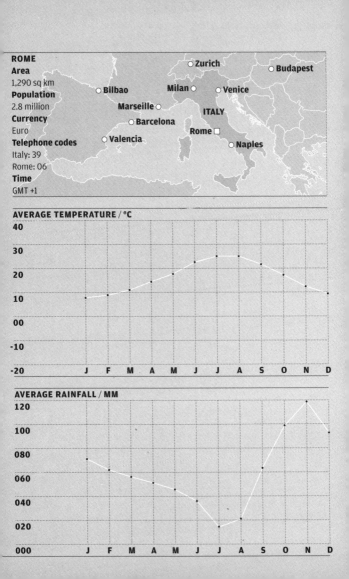

ROME

Area
1,290 sq km

Population
2.8 million

Currency
Euro

Telephone codes
Italy: 39
Rome: 06

Time
GMT +1

Zurich ○   ● Budapest

○ Bilbao   Milan ○   ○ Venice

Marseille ○   **ITALY**

○ Barcelona   Rome □

○ Valencia   ○ Naples

AVERAGE TEMPERATURE / °C

	J	F	M	A	M	J	J	A	S	O	N	D

40
30
20
10
00
-10
-20

J F M A M J J A S O N D

AVERAGE RAINFALL / MM

120
100
080
060
040
020
000

J F M A M J J A S O N D

NEIGHBOURHOODS
THE AREAS YOU NEED TO KNOW AND WHY

To help you navigate the city, we've chosen the most interesting districts (see below and the map inside the back cover) and colour-coded our featured venues, according to their location; those venues that are outside these areas are not coloured.

CENTRO STORICO
The Pantheon (see p010) is the historic centre's ancient icon, but Piazza Navona (see p034), where rivals Bernini and Borromini tried to outdo each other with baroque basilicas and ornate fountains, is just as impressive. Campo de' Fiori is worth a pitstop for a slice of *pizza bianca*.

PIGNETO
This area is shedding its working-class image, represented in so many neorealist films, and becoming the city's hedonistic hub. Young creatives flock here, attracted by the low rents, loft spaces and nightlife, at venues such as Primo (see p059) and Fanfulla 101 (Via Fanfulla da Lodi 101).

ANCIENT ROME
The statue of a wolf suckling Romulus and Remus is housed in the Capitoline Museums, which stand around the edges of Piazza del Campidoglio. Adjacent is the Roman Forum, which was the epicentre of the ancient empire. But the majesty of the Colosseum (see p012) is more arresting.

MONTI AND ESQUILINO
The area around Esquilino, one of Rome's seven hills, is the city's most multi-ethnic district. Esquilino itself might still be rough around the edges compared to hip Monti, but a renovation of its modernist Termini station (see p011) has helped turn around its fortunes. If in the area try the organic restaurant Urban 47 (see p041).

TRASTEVERE
So-called because it lies across the River Tiber, Trastevere was once the bohemian quarter of Rome. Although it still has an arty edge, it is now largely home to well-heeled expats. The area comes alive at night, when its cafés, such as Il Baretto (see p058), fill up with locals and tourists.

TRIDENTE
Surrounded by classical statuary, Piazza del Popolo sits at the heart of Tridente. Three roads lead off it: Via di Ripetta, Via del Corso and Via del Babuino, which ends at the Spanish Steps. Above it sprawls the green space of the Villa Borghese, Rome's most popular public park.

TESTACCIO
Monte Testaccio is not one of the famous seven hills, but an ancient rubbish tip made up of shards of discarded amphorae. A draw for its nightlife, the area's clubs and bars sparked off the inevitable process of gentrification, which has also crept into the neighbouring district of Ostiense.

VIA VENETO
Via Vittorio Veneto was one of the stars of the seminal 1960 film *La Dolce Vita*. It lost its cachet years ago, but a revival which began in 2003, with the opening of the Aleph (see p020), has been upheld with a string of swish eateries. To the south is Palazzo Barberini and to the west is the Trevi Fountain.

LANDMARKS

THE SHAPE OF THE CITY SKYLINE

Ever get the feeling you know a city without having been there? Thanks to the glut of films (*La Dolce Vita*, *Three Coins in the Fountain*, *Quo Vadis* et al) set in Rome in the 25 years after Vittorio De Sica's *Bicycle Thieves* of 1948, the city exists as a distinct and unwavering tableau in the popular psyche. You won't see Audrey Hepburn hitch up her frock and climb on a Vespa in Piazza Navona, nor a toga-togged Charlton Heston smuggling cappuccinos to lepers in the catacombs, but you will certainly encounter a considerable visual familiarity at almost every turn. And, as anyone who has set foot on these seven illustrious hills will confirm, the basic cinematic assumptions are no distortion. As a consequence, navigating the city should be easy. There are impressive reference points everywhere, although they are often obscured by tourists.

Everyone has their own method for dealing with the madness that is Rome in full summer swing. We have three. Santa Sabina's Basilica (Via Santa Sabina) and its neighbouring churches on the verdant Aventine offer a fabulous peephole view of St Peter's Basilica (see p015). Make sure too that you tackle Rome's best sights, such as the Vatican Museums (Viale Vaticano, T 06 6988 3860), on your Vespa – it's the only way to see them in a day. And however tight your schedule, leave time to take a *gelato* on a *passeggiata* around Piazza Navona (see p034) before bed. *For full addresses, see Resources.*

Pantheon

When the Emperor Hadrian gave the go-ahead for this ancient temple to be rebuilt with its now-famous poured-concrete dome, he couldn't have predicted that this would be the building by which posterity would remember him. In many ways, the structure isn't a success: the proportions of the building are out of synch, notably the enormous pediment, which squats, toad-like, over impossibly delicate Corinthian columns. The other famous aberration is that, incredibly, the unreinforced concrete dome hasn't collapsed – even the very latest concrete construction techniques would not be able to replicate the feat that Hadrian's builders achieved in the 2nd century AD.

Piazza della Rotonda, T 06 6830 0230

Termini station

For a long time, Rome's Esquiline hill was the home of one of its shabbiest neighbourhoods. That has been changing over the past few years and the district is now one of the city's most interesting, if still untypically Roman and rather rough around the edges. At its heart is the impressive Termini station, which was started in 1942 to complement Mussolini's satellite city of exhibition halls called Esposizione Universale Romana, or EUR (see p068). Completed in the 1960s, the 232m-long front elevation and concrete canopy have earned it the nickname of 'the dinosaur', and make for an interesting mix of Fascist and modern architecture.
Piazza dei Cinquecento

Colosseum

For years, it was left largely to fend for itself – just another Roman ruin in a city already lousy with them, the Colosseum was chiefly memorable for the legions of touts it attracted. But that all changed in 2000 when a massive redevelopment programme was started. The floor was restored, everything was tidied up and they started charging for admission.
Piazza del Colosseo, T 06 3996 7700

Aventine post office

It seems downright unfair, given the fact that Rome is so well endowed with architectural treasures, that even a local post office can attract enthusiasts in their droves. This is a landmark, not just in happening Testaccio, but in the history of Italian rationalism. Completed in 1935, and designed by Adalberto Libera and Mario de Renzi, the building displays all the imperial posturing consistent with the local interpretation of this style of architecture. They don't make post offices like this anymore, more's the pity, and it's hard to remember quite why they ever did. But if you have to waste valuable time on minor administrative chores, here would be a great place to do it, and you'll struggle to find a more amenable crowd.

Palazzo delle Poste all' Aventino, Via Marmorata

St Peter's Basilica

Watching the locals and the tourists in Rome is like going to the theatre. And at the Vatican, it's a high-camp performance. Take the celebrated garb of the Swiss Guard. They might be a *bona fide* papal protection force, but with the best will in the world, they are never going to look like a crack military unit in red, yellow and blue pedal-pushers. But then, the artists and architects of the baroque were also masters in staged effects. None more so than Gian Lorenzo Bernini, whose creations now frame a million calendars and fashion shoots. His colonnades at St Peter's can sometimes seem like the best place, and certainly the easiest, to experience his work.

Piazza San Pietro, www.vatican.va

HOTELS

WHERE TO STAY AND WHICH ROOMS TO BOOK

Although the undisputed destination for discerning travellers to Italy, Rome trailed for decades behind the great capitals of the world in offering chic, design-led accommodation. The two top-end choices, the Hotel Hassler (Piazza della Trinità dei Monti 6, T 06 699 340) and the Hotel Eden (Via Ludovisi 49, T 06 478 121), which are both perched above the Spanish Steps, dominated the luxury market and dazzled starlets, politicos and the international jet set with the stunning views from their top-floor restaurants. However, even post-renovation, these grandes dames feel dated.

After Rocco Forte's stylish Hotel de Russie (see p026) opened in 2000, a new generation of hotels led Roman hospitality into the 21st century. Fashion dynasties Ferragamo and Fendi tapped into the market, the former with the Portrait Suites (see p024), the latter with Villa Laetitia (see p028) and Tre Pupazzi (Via dei Tre Pupazzi 4, T 06 322 6776), whereas architect Richard Meier revamped a floor of politicians' haunt, the Raphael Hotel (Largo Febo 2, T 06 682 831). For a compromise between stuffy classics and brash newcomers, try the St George (see p030), a Wallpaper* Best Business Hotel 2008, Fortyseven (Via Luigi Petroselli 47, T 06 678 7816), with its art deco-inspired interior and floors dedicated to 20th-century Italian art, or Hotel Capo d'Africa (Via Capo d'Africa 54, T 06 772 801), in the shadow of the Colosseum (see p012). *For full addresses and room rates, see Resources.*

Leon's Place

The new kid on the block in terms of design hotels, Leon's Place is a stone's throw from Termini station and not far from the Museum of Contemporary Art. Designed by Hotelphilosophy, it has comfy rooms with French beds and neutral tones. The public areas feature a more dramatic look with crystal chandeliers, draped curtains, stucco columns and day beds. All rooms come with mod cons and glittering mosaic bathrooms, a theme reflected in the cocktail bar area, with its blue mosaic counter. Opt for a Junior Suite (above). The Hotel also offers wellbeing treatments, valet parking and a large conference area.

Via XX Settembre 90/94, T 06 890 871, www.leonsplace.com

Lobby, Leon's Place

Aleph

The devilishly dark red lobby, bar and restaurant of this hotel, designed by Adam D Tihany, are supposed to be inspired by a hellish motif that contrasts with the bright bedrooms, which evoke 'heaven'. Perhaps these are not the wisest of themes for a hotel, but other playful statements, such as the hologram bookcases in the library, the giant dice suspended over a backgammon-board floor in the central courtyard (above) and the film stills that line the lifts, make the Aleph a favourite with the fashion set. The Junior Suite is a 1970s playboy's dream in zebrano wood, but we recommend booking one of the Deluxe Rooms; those on the fourth floor have balconies and good views. *Via di San Basilio 15, T 06 422 901, www.aleph.boscolohotels.com*

Il Palazzetto

If you're in the mood for a little *Roman Holiday*-style romance, check in to one of the three rooms at Il Palazzetto that look on to the Spanish Steps — they are all sold at the same rate but vary in décor and layout; our favourite is Room 2. Tripping lightly down the magnificent spiral staircase (above) en route to the boutiques of Via dei Condotti will inspire an Audrey Hepburn moment, dampened only by the sight of the McDonald's adjacent to the tiny reception. Enjoy an *aperitivo* at Il Palazzetto restaurant's illuminated retro bar, before sampling chef Vincenzo di Tuoro's innovative cooking and a bottle from the 400-strong wine list.
Vicolo del Bottino 8, T 06 699 341 000, www.ilpalazzettoroma.com

Casa Manni

Armano Manni has built a reputation among gourmands and celebrities thanks to his award-winning Manni extra-virgin olive oils. To respond to the requests of his starry clientele, he opened a retreat to provide a glimpse of the authentic Roman lifestyle, without foregoing the five-star treatment. Designed by Adam D Tihany, Casa Manni is a penthouse for two, located in a 17th-century palazzo overlooking the column of Marcus Aurelius. Guests have access to the owner's little black book, packed with tips and the finest addresses in Rome, and can select a bottle from Manni's impressive cellar of more than 1,000 bottles, or just relax on the terrace or living room (above), leafing through the art books on display.
Via di Pietra 70, T 06 9727 4787,
www.casamanni.com

Hotel Locarno

This delightful and popular pied-à-terre has a distinctively Italianate charm. Each of the 66 rooms has been individually decorated, either with hand-printed art deco-style wallpaper or tapestries, and all are furnished with original Liberty lamps. The choice of reservation is crucial, as standards vary hugely. The building across from the bar and breakfast *terrazza* has rooms that are bigger and better value; the most spectacular are the Venetian Suite (above) and the equally decadent but slightly smaller Rooms 602 and 605. Opened in May 2009, the in-house Salotto Locarno is a gorgeous spot for a cocktail. If you can't get a reservation here, try its nearby sister hotel, the 19-room Anahi (T 06 361 0841). *Via della Penna 22, T 06 361 0841, www.hotellocarno.com*

Portrait Suites

A luxury Roman townhouse is the concept
behind this intimate hotel, opened by
the Ferragamo-owned Lungarno group
in 2006. As you would expect from such
a fashion pedigree, the hotel is peppered
with footwear-related sketches and black-
and-white photos, oversized mirrors and
dashes of modish lime and cyclamen pink.
There are few public spaces in the hotel;
even breakfast is room service only, the
idea being that you can luxuriate in the
comfort of your own spacious suite and
call upon the attentive staff to satisfy your
every whim. The five studios, eight suites
and penthouse (right) are all equipped
with satellite TV, DVD players, wi-fi and
kitchenettes. We particularly like the
rooftop terrace, where you can sip a drink
on comfy sofas in front of an open fire.
*Via Bocca di Leone 23, T 06 6938 0742,
www.rome-suites-portrait.com*

Hotel de Russie

The choice of many celebrities, politicians and artists – Cocteau and Picasso stayed here – the Russie's landscaped gardens (left), complete with Roman ruins and views of the Villa Borghese, are legendary, and its terrace bar, serving cocktails and sandwiches, is a society hot spot in summer. The façade is as discreet as the service, and the hotel's elegant interiors should ensure that the Russie ages gracefully. Bond-style martinis are served at Bar Stravinskij, and the hotel's spa is one of the best in town. Book into a Double Deluxe Room (above), or if you have more to spend, the Popolo Suite, for its stunning views of the eponymous Piazza.
Via del Babuino 9, T 06 328 881, www.hotelderussie.it

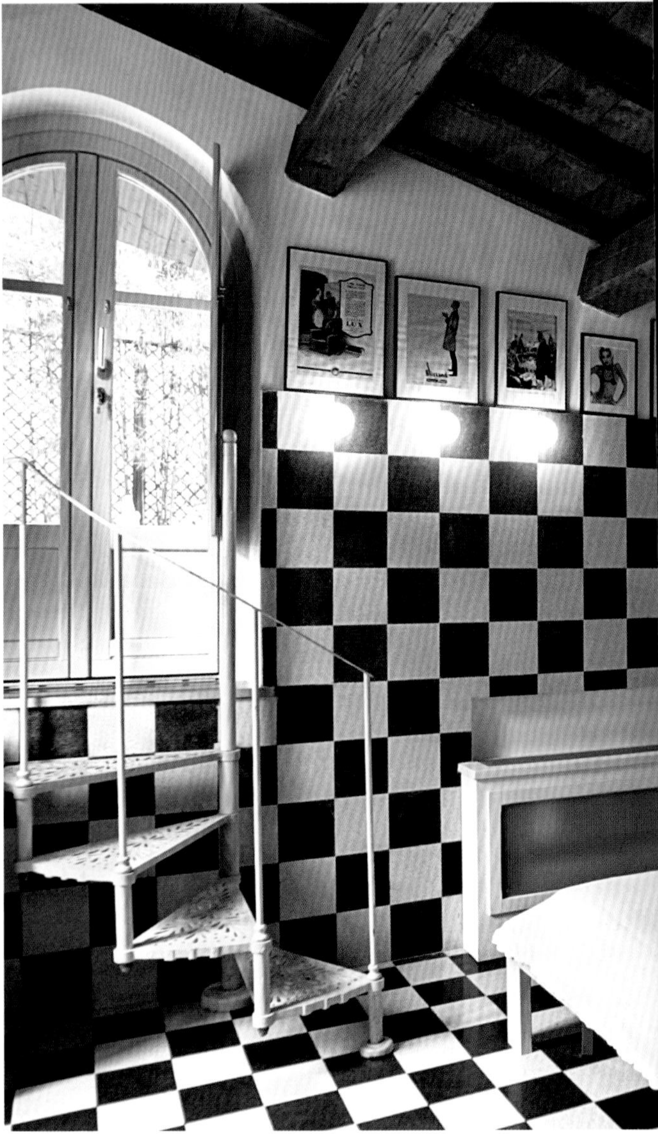

Villa Laetitia
It sits just off a Tiber-side road, but this 1911 villa is a peaceful retreat set amid a lush garden. Owned by Anna Fendi Venturini and her two daughters, it has 15 individually designed rooms, most with a terrace or garden access. Check in to the Karl Room, dedicated to Herr Lagerfeld, or the Atelier Suite (pictured). *Lungotevere delle Armi 22-23, T 06 322 6776, www.villalaetitia.com*

030

St George

Set against the 16th-century backdrop of Via Giulia, St George opened in 2007 and is a haven for lovers of understated chic. Architect Lorenzo Bellini quotes Alvar Aalto and Arne Jacobsen as inspirations for the interior that is decorated with muted tones and minimalist furnishings, as in the Junior Suite 218 (pictured).

Via Giulia 62, T 06 686 611,
www.stgeorgehotel.it

24 HOURS
SEE THE BEST OF THE CITY IN JUST ONE DAY

Pacing yourself in Rome is paramount, as cultural overload can bring on Stendhal syndrome, which causes fainting and hallucinations – even confirmed atheists will be dazzled by the paintings and sculptures housed in the city's ecclesiastical gems. Despite the rather showy opulence of St Peter's (see p015), Michelangelo's dome and his iconic Pietà are worth a peek, before visiting the Sistine Chapel and Raphael's rooms in the Vatican Museums (Viale Vaticano, T 06 6988 3860). The baroque San Carlo alle Quattro Fontane (Via del Quirinale 23, T 06 488 3261) is testament to the genius of Francesco Borromini, while the architectural palimpsest of the Basilica di San Clemente (Piazza San Clemente) spans three eras of Roman history. Also visit the Chiesa di Sant' Ignazio di Loyola (Via del Caravita 8a, T 06 679 4406), after admiring the Renaissance masterpieces at the Galleria Doria Pamphilj (Piazza del Collegio Romano 2, T 06 679 7323).

Other noteworthy art galleries include Centrale Montemartini (Via Ostiense 106, T 06 574 8042), Palazzo delle Esposizioni (see p038), MACRO (opposite), which was extended in 2008 by Odile Decq, and MACRO Future (Piazza Orazio Giustiniani 4). Zaha Hadid's MAXXI art museum (see p065) now snakes across the skyline, while Massimiliano Fuksas's futuristic congress centre, Cloud, should be completed by 2011.

For full addresses, see Resources.

10.00 MACRO

MACRO's new wing by architect Odile Decq provides the museum with a 3,000 sq m roof garden, which doubles as a public space, a retractable roof and a central 400 sq m fountain, all built in steel and glass, and punctuated by black and red glossy structures. Inside, the collection displays works by Carla Accardi, Mimmo Rotella and Pino Pascali, as well as younger Italian artists like Paolo Canevari. New pieces on extended loan include works by Lucio Fontana and Cindy Sherman. To get a taste of the whole collection you should also visit MACRO Future in the Testaccio area. Inside the old slaughterhouse two pavilions have been restored to host exhibitions by the younger generation of artists. *Via Reggio Emilia 54, T 06 671 070 400, www.macro.roma.museum*

12.00 Piazza Navona

Before lunch at Cul de Sac (overleaf), take a stroll around the open-air baroque masterpiece, Piazza Navona, and its basilica Sant'Agnese (pictured). Then after lunch hop on the 116 electric bus to Via del Tritone and head for Il Gelato di San Crispino (T 06 679 3924) on Via della Panetteria. Order the signature wild Sardinian honey flavour and savour your *coppa* in front of the Trevi Fountain.

13.00 Cul de Sac

The space might be a little cosy (the restaurant is long, narrow and always packed), but the convivial atmosphere and modest prices make Cul de Sac an ideal stop, especially for a light but lingering lunch. The menu has meats and cheeses, all from immaculate sources. There are also Middle Eastern-influenced side dishes, such as baba ganoush, soups and the freshest Greek salad in town.

Choose from around 90 wines available by the glass and 1,500 bottles, on a wine list of epic proportions.
Piazza Pasquino 73, T 06 6880 1094, web.tiscali.it/culdesac

16.00 Stadio dei Marmi

If Bernini's baroque statuary is poetry in stone, then the 60 figures that circle this athletics stadium are utopian masculinity in marble, in the style of an Armani ad. Commissioned by Mussolini in the 1920s – and designed by Enrico Del Debbio – the stadium was finally inagurated in 1932. Each of the classical oversized nudes represents both a sport and a province of Italy. As an addition to the Academy of

Physical Education the aim was to inspire a strong, healthy Italian youth.
Viale del Foro Italico, T 06 324 0334

17.00 Open Colonna

For a contemporary end to your day
in Rome, head to Open Colonna, the
restaurant at the Palazzo delle Esposizioni
art gallery. Designed by Pio Piacentini
in 1883, it was renovated in 2007 by
architect Firouz Galdo as part of a project
by Michele De Lucchi. The 3,000 sq m
exhibition space is spread over two levels
in a series of immaculate white stucco
exhibition rooms. The glass-covered
restaurant was created by architect
Paolo Desideri and features furniture by
Cappellini, including Marc Newson 'Felt'
chairs and 'Orgone' tables. Here, diners
can feast on chef Antonello Colonna's
clever reinventions of Roman classics.
Colonna's former restaurant in Labico,
49km south of the city, was a renowned
foodie destination, and his Rome opening
remains a hot spot for gourmands.
*Palazzo delle Esposizioni, Via Milano 9a,
T 06 4782 2641, www.opencolonna.it*

URBAN LIFE
CAFÉS, RESTAURANTS, BARS AND NIGHTCLUBS

Even though Rome's dining scene is becoming more fashionable by the week, it would be a shame to miss out on a simple dish of *spaghetti al pomodoro e basilico* at a traditional trattoria such as Checco er Carrettiere (Via Benedetta 10, T 06 580 0985). To refuel during a cultural marathon around Centro Storico, stop at Forno Campo de' Fiori (Campo de' Fiori 22, T 06 6880 6662) for a slice of *pizza bianca* (pizza bread seasoned with olive oil and sea salt). Metodo Classico (Via Guglielmo Calderini 64, T 06 324 4262) serves fresh fish in modern surroundings, or try to get a table at Le Mani in Pasta (Via dei Genovesi 37, T 06 581 6017), a Trastevere favourite and one of the best affordable restaurants in town.

For a casual glass of wine mid-shopping spree, visit Ai Tre Scalini Bottiglieria (Via Panisperna 251, T 06 4890 7495) in the emerging area of Monti; enjoy an *aperitivo* lounging on faded vintage sofas at Mister Pucci (Piazza Mastai 18); or mingle with artists and art curators at Camponeschi (Piazza Farnese 50, T 06 687 4927). A reliable address for live music, Circolo degli Artisti (Via Casilinia Vecchia 42, T 06 7030 5684) in Pigneto always attracts fun crowds. Alternatively, head south towards Testaccio and Ostiense where La Saponeria (Via degli Argonauti 20, T 06 574 6999), Akab (Via di Monte Testaccio 69, T 06 5725 0585) and Rising Love (Via delle Conce 14) pull in the coolest crowds.
For full addresses, see Resources.

Urbana 47

If you want to taste Rome's best organic, locally sourced, seasonal produce then Urbana 47 and sister restaurant Zoc (T 06 6819 2515) should be at the top of your list. Urban 47's menu lists the source of each ingredient used in its dishes, and features delicacies such as anchovies, fennel and broad bean terrine. If the vintage period décor also takes your fancy then feel free to order it to go, since most of the pieces are for sale. Brunch on Sundays is a popular and affordable family affair, where you can often spot the chefs making fresh pasta on the marble tables. *Via Urbana 47, T 06 4788 4006, www.urbana47.it*

Molto

Located in the Parioli district, this restaurant/café/emporium attracts an upmarket clientele. Architect Iunio Cellini converted the 320 sq m warehouse into several spacious rooms. In the main dining area, huge windows open on to a leafy terrace, a lovely spot for a sundowner. Neutral tones lend the interior a relaxed, elegant feel, and the contemporary Italian cooking is equally unfussy. The cellar is packed with well-chosen wines and there are plenty of foodie delights for sale, such as olive oils, chocolate, marinated artichokes and chillies, and a selection of culinary tomes. *Viale Parioli 122, T 06 808 2900, www.moltoitaliano.it*

Caffè della Pace

It might not have the contemporary design kudos of many of its neighbouring bars, but if you're looking for a taste of traditional Roman culture, head here. Framed by a climbing vine and located next door to Bramante's 16th-century cloister, Caffè della Pace, which opened in 1891, is the place to sit and watch the world go by while enjoying a delicious *caffè shakerato* (iced espresso, which can be given numerous house twists). The dark interior, with its large mirrors and marble and mahogany counter, is a seductive spot for a tête-à-tête and an evening of romantic cocktail-sipping. *Via della Pace 3-7, T 06 686 1216, www.caffedellapace.it*

Bar Necci

Opened in 1924 as an ice-cream parlour by brothers Pietro and Luigi Necci, this was one of the locations for Pier Paolo Pasolini's 1961 film *Accattone*, a gritty depiction of life in Rome's slums. In the 1960s, Bar Necci became the epicentre of Pigneto's social life and the current owners have played on its retro appeal to turn it into a hip destination once again. Like so many contemporary urban haunts, this is a multifunctional venue, kicking off with breakfast, then ending the day as a late-night bar. Its menu, printed on old, faded comic sheets, features dishes such as a salad of raw artichokes with Parmesan shavings, and barley wheat with courgette flowers. In summer, the garden is packed with young local trendsetters.
Via Fanfulla da Lodi 68, T 06 9760 1552, www.necci1924.com

Salotto Locarno

Cashing in on Hotel Locarno's intimate and hip reputation, Salotto Locarno, the bar located on the hotel's ground floor, is a favourite for 1920 style cocktails and delicious finger food. The art deco style, roaring fireplace and Tiffany lamps make it a cosy hide-away spot during the winter, and the vine-clad outdoor terrace has packed tables from May onwards. If you're still feeling peckish, continue the evening at the in-house restaurant, opened in 2010. As with its sister venue Salotto 42 (Piazza di Pietra) and the summer-only, street art cafè Salotto Gianicolo, Salotto Locarno attracts a fashionable mix of well-heeled Romans and celebrities.
Via della Penna 22, T 06 361 0841, www.hotellocarno.com

Tree Bar

Set in the middle of a small park in Flaminio, this former kiosk has been converted into a vibrant meeting spot. A Scandinavian-inspired interior with 1950s-style furniture and lighting is encased in a wood-and-glass external shell. Open from 6pm until 1am, Tree Bar serves Mediterranean dishes and homemade cakes, and is a popular late-night stop for concert-goers from the nearby Auditorium Parco della Musica (see p070). During the summer you may catch a music event or DJ set taking place in the garden.
Via Flaminia 226, T 06 3265 2754

Ristorante Angelina

Located in Testaccio, Angelina is endowed with great terraces, which host happy hours and dancing nights during the summer. The menu is mainly meat-based, but you can also order pizzas from the wood oven. Many restaurants in Testaccio serve a cuisine inspired by the nearby slaughterhouse. Not for the fainthearted, classic recipes in this area include oxtail stew, pasta with sweetbreads and tripe.

Since you are in the neighbourhood, do check out the local institution Checchino dal 1887 (Via Monte Testaccio 30, T 06 574 3816) and the always crowded Da Felice (Via Mastro Giorgio 29, T 06 574 6800). *Via Galvani 24a, T 06 5728 3840 www.ristoranteangelina.com*

Ristorante Angelina

Pastificio San Lorenzo

Since opening in September 2009, this restaurant has quickly established a reputation as the place to see and be seen at in Rome. Located in an old warehouse, which now houses artist studios, it maintains an impeccable artistic pedigree thanks to the collectors who own it and the buzzing crowd of gallerists, thespians and beautiful people who typically grace the tables. The décor is by Roberto Liorni, of Primo (see p059) fame, and features an open kitchen and a long metal counter on which one can enjoy snacks of Parma ham and a glass or two of Franciacorta bubbly. The restaurant menu ranges from hamburger on black squid ink bread, to tempura fried shrimps. Befriend the charming manager Alino, for a good table and for a suggestion from the excellent wine list.

Via Tiburtina 196, T 06 9727 3519, www.pastificiocerere.com

Obikà

Designed by Roman studio Labics, Obikà (which means 'here it is' in the Neapolitan dialect) is a mozzarella bar that has been given a Japanese edge. Perch on a stool at the sushi-bar-style counter and sample the top-quality Mozzarella di Bufala Campana from Paestum and Agro Pontino, delivered daily. Alternatively, linger over the Italian menu in the larger dining area (above). The layers of wood-oven-baked bread with buffalo ricotta, smoked wild salmon and chickpea cream is a favourite. Obikà also boasts a strong Italian wine list. A second branch is located in Campo de' Fiori (T 06 6880 2366).
Via dei Prefetti 26, T 06 683 2630, www.obika.it

SAID Chocolate Factory

This 1923 chocolate factory, just outside the city walls in San Lorenzo, was converted into a laboratory/shop/café in 2006 and is now a point of pilgrimage for Rome's chocoholics. The retro furniture and wall displays of original mills, copper basins and steel moulds warm up the airy industrial spaces. The chocolate, which is exhibited in jars and stylish packaging on the large communal counter tables, comes in the form of ricotta-cheese pralines, truffles, chocolate made with Himalayan pink salt and a thick, *gianduia* chocolate spread. Other chocolate hot spots in town are Confetteria Moriondo e Gariglio (T 06 699 0856), founded in 1886, and La Bottega del Cioccolato (T 06 482 1473). SAID is closed from mid-June to the end of August.
Via Tiburtina 135, T 06 446 9204

La Casa del Caffè Tazza d'Oro

La Tazza d'Oro (The Golden Cup) has been offering the quintessential Roman breakfast of a creamy cappuccino and a sweet, crisp *cornetto* since it opened in the 1940s. In summer, order a *granita di caffè*, a sort of iced coffee served with cream. You can also buy packets of the legendary house blend, Regina dei Caffè. *Via dei Orfani 84, T 06 678 9792, www.tazzadorocoffeeshop.com*

Il Baretto

In sharp contrast to the early 19th-century buildings in the leafier part of Trastevere, this café/bar is housed in a suspended metal-and-glass cube, designed by Roman architects Morq. An American marble counter and cement floor are offset by the retro tables and chairs, and 1950s jukebox, which featured in Nanni Moretti's 1984 cult Italian film *Bianca*. Owners Richard and Allegra Ercolani have long been a fixture on the Roman dance scene as DJs and event organisers, so it's no surprise to learn that Il Baretto's forte is its music, which ranges from jazz to old and new rock. Order a Campari cocktail, such as the Spritz or Americano, and kick back on the spacious terrace overlooking the city. The venue is open from 7.30am until 2am.
Via Garibaldi 27g

Primo

Since its launch in late 2006, Primo has won two Gambero Rosso awards and has become one of the hottest tables in town, putting the Pigneto area firmly on the map. Owned by ex-'Gusto chef Marco Gallotta, the founding owner of Crudo (Via degli Specchi 6, T 06 683 8989) Massimo Terzulli and jewellery designer Roberta Paolucci of Iosselliani (see p078), Primo's constantly changing menu is creative modern Italian cooking at its best. You can also come here for a preprandial spumante and tapas-style snacks. After dinner, Primo draws a lively, arty crowd to its bar. For further imaginative cooking, try Il Pagliaccio (T 06 6880 9595) in Centro Storico, whose kitchen is headed by chef Anthony Genovese.
Via del Pigneto 46, T 06 701 3827, www.primoalpigneto.it

Tati al 28

Part of 'Gusto's gastronomic empire,
Tatì al 28 is inspired by French bistros
and brasseries, and offers dishes such
as spaghetti with clams and grilled
goat cheese with radicchio in the
upstairs restaurant (pictured). The
atmosphere downstairs is clubby,
with dj sets from 7pm until midnight.
Piazza Augusto Imperatore 28,
T 06 6813 4221, www.gusto.it

INSIDER'S GUIDE
LIVIA RISI, FASHION DESIGNER

Fashion designer Livia Risi (www.liviarisi.it) creates slinky, jersey dresses and tops from her Trastevere boutique La Ciumachella (Via dei Vascellari 37, T 06 5830 1667). Her transformer dress, cut so it can be arranged in at least ten different ways, is a firm favourite among the Roman aristo-boho crowd.

Risi's day starts with a cappuccino from Terra Satis (Piazza dei Ponziani 1a, T 06 9760 3734), which used to be one of the favourite haunts of Italian film director and writer Pier Paolo Pasolini. For lunch she might head to the chic Parioli area of town and have a snack at Annibale Vini & Spiriti (Piazza Dei Carracci 4, T 06 322 3835), or a meal at Orlando (Via Mantova 5/b, T 06 8535 5542), which specialises in Sicilian delicacies such as swordfish and almond pastries. Like a true Trastevere local, she stops for coffee or ice cream at Bar San Calisto (Piazza San Calisto 4, T 06 5835 869).

'I only use Italian textiles for my creations,' says Risi. For vintage silks, Livia scours flea market Porta Portese, or searches for samples in the old textile shops that line Via dei Falegnami in the Jewish Ghetto. She usually takes her *aperitivo* at B-Gallery (see p086) and Lettere e Caffé (Via Francesco a Ripa, T 06 9727 0991) for slam poetry competitions. For late night dancing, it's off to Rashomon (Via degli Argonauti 16, T 347 340 5710), a small, underground club specialising in minimal techno, electronica and house music.
For full addresses, see Resources.

ARCHITOUR
A GUIDE TO ROME'S ICONIC BUILDINGS

The summer streets of the Eternal City are littered with the dehydrated bodies of those poor, sun-touched tourists who tried to take in every last bit of its Renaissance architecture and art, ideally before lunchtime. Those few souls who survive into the afternoon for a tour of the city's classical treasures are typically rendered catatonic long before it's time for an *aperitivo*. In short, Rome can defeat even the most indefatigable architourist. Here, there really is no shame in admitting that too much is not always a good thing. We've already helped you artfully plant your pumps around a choice smattering of the city's mainstream jewels in our guide to Rome's landmarks (see p009), so now we are going to assume you are ready for a modestly paced antidote to the city's well-worn (but still unmissable) grand tour.

That Mussolini had big plans for Rome is widely known. Quite how far he got with them can be a surprise. He aimed to build a satellite city south of Via Ostiense that would link Rome to the sea and serve as a monument to Fascism. Work on the Esposizione Universale Romana (EUR) ground to a halt during WWII, but resumed after Il Duce's death, when a modernist flavour was added to his cocktail of Fascist monumentalism. Combine a viewing with a visit to some modern treasures and you have a Roman experience touching those places where the *Blue Guide* fears to tread.
For full addresses, see Resources.

Maxxi

When Maxxi finally opened in May 2010 after a decade in the making, a crowd of 50,000 hungry art lovers flocked to see it during the first 48 hours. This Zaha Hadid building strikes a dramatic note against the baroque Roman skyline. The collection is still a young one but takes pride in displaying works by Anish Kapoor, Gilbert and George, Maurizio Cattelan, Gerhard Richter, Vanessa Beecroft and Gino De Dominicis. The museum also houses architectural archives, drawings and photography. Located in the Flaminio district, Maxxi is within walking distance of the Auditorium Parco della Musica (see p070).
Maxxi, Via Guido Reni 4, T 06 321 0181, www.maxxi.beniculturali.it

Entrance hall, Maxxi

Palazzo della Civiltà del Lavoro

Giovanni Guerrini's Palazzo is referred to by locals as the Colosseo Quadrato (Square Colosseum), thanks to its six floors of arcades that mimic the ancient monument. Its dominant location on the Tiber and its dramatic statuary have made it the symbol of Esposizione Universale Romana (EUR). In the same complex, the architecture of Adalberto Libera's Museo della Civiltà Romana (T 06 06 08), in Piazza Giovanni Agnelli, is a synthesis of modern styles with a classical inspiration. The museum's collection includes plaster casts of Roman treasures scattered around the world and an enormous model of Rome at the time of Constantine.
Esposizione Universale Romana (EUR)

Accademia di Danimarca

For a break from Rome's architectural past, visit the Accademia di Danimarca, Danish architect Kay Fisker's 1967 homage to his homeland. The building was funded by the Carlsberg family to promote Danish culture in Italy, so it's perhaps no surprise to see that its shuns Roman grandiosity completely in favour of a resolutely Scandinavian style. Although once a controversial presence, the gentle, geometric building clad in pale yellow brick now seems settled into the surroundings of the leafy parkland of Villa Borghese. The academy displays Danish art and craft, holds concerts and welcomes visitors to its 24,000-book library.
Via Omero 18, T 06 326 5931, www.dkinst-rom.dk

Auditorium Parco della Musica
A choral extravaganza in surround
sound at Renzo Piano's acoustically
perfect auditorium is a great way to
while away an evening. If you haven't
got time to see a show, just admire
the exteriors of these three beetle-like
buildings, which mix wood, stone and
organic curves to excellent effect.
Viale Pietro de Coubertin 15,
T 06 8024 1281, www.auditorium.com

SHOPPING
THE BEST RETAIL THERAPY AND WHAT TO BUY

Via del Corso and the roads that lead off it are the city's retail epicentre, full of one-off boutiques and big brands such as Gucci (see p076). For a good selection of Italian labels, head for the unisex stores Gente (Via Frattina 69, T 06 678 9132) and Degli Effetti (Piazza Capranica 75, 79 and 93, T 06 679 0202). Stock up on bikinis and kaftans at Laura Urbinati (Via dei Banchi Vecchi 50a, T 06 6813 6478), or commission an exquisitely crafted leather handbag or briefcase at Federico Polidori (Via del Piè di Marmo 7, T 06 679 7191). For modern interior design, Spazio Sette (Via dei Barbieri 7, T 06 686 9747) and Loto Design (Via Filippo Civinini 39, T 06 3600 6879) are two of our picks. Alternatively, hunt for 1950s and 1960s Scandinavian and Italian pieces at reasonable prices at Attik (Via Giovanni Battista Tiepolo 18, T 06 9761 1053).

Via del Governo Vecchio buzzes with bars, boutiques and retro shops like Vestiti Usati Cinzia (No 45, T 06 683 2945). Trastevere is more idiosyncratic. Here, Scala Quattordici (Via della Scala 13-14, T 06 588 3580) makes tailored suits and silk dresses, whereas B-Gallery (see p086) is a modish bookstore/café/exhibition space. Vintage fans should seek out clothing at the Via Sannio market (Monday to Saturday), antiques at the Borghetto Flaminio market (Piazzale della Marina 32, Sundays) and books and prints along Largo della Fontanella di Borghese (Monday to Saturday).

For full addresses, see Resources.

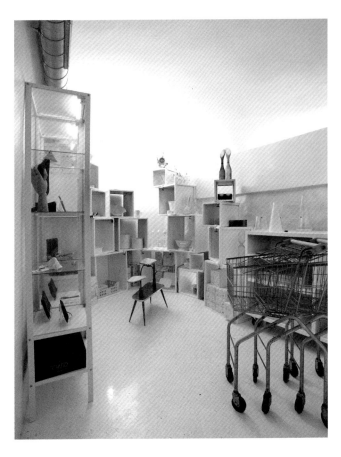

Super

Super's subdued all-white entrance does not do justice to the treasure trove of menswear and womenswear labels located in the vaulted rooms downstairs. Step down a few steps and you will find all the necessary ingredients to create the 'Monti' area look so popular on the streets outside, made from a discerning mix of vintage, hip and lesser known North European brands such as Margit

Brandt. Retro Italian, Danish furniture and accessories from the 1950s and 1970s blend with new designers' pieces and the white walls also play host to exhibitions and art book launches. Those looking for a quirky gift should snap up the map dishes by Italian ceramic manufacturer Seletti. *Via Leonina 42, T 06 9826 6450, www.super-space.com*

Motel Salieri
This menswear boutique is a refined
haven miles away from the high street
shopping experience. Partner Fabio
Quaranta started his career at Rome's
top fashion stores and then graduated
to designing clothes. In 2010, his latest
label FQR won the Who is on Next
award at Pitti Uomo Florence.
Via Giovanni Lanza 162, T 06 4898 9966
www.motelsalieri.com

Gucci

Redesigned by Gucci's creative director, Frida Giannini, the label's Rome flagship store has been restored to its 1960s glory. Gone are the brassy logo and brash 1990s feel in favour of a subtler aesthetic. The doorman provides old-school glamour, and the full range of bags, sunglasses and jewellery is showcased. While you're in town, don't miss Valentino (womenswear, T 06 679 5862; menswear, T 06 673 9285) and Brioni (T 06 484 517). A good selection of Belgian labels displayed among a collection of ceramic vases by Ettore Sottsass for Memphis can be found at L'Una e L'Altra's shop at Piazza Pasquino 76 (T 06 6880 4995). *Via dei Condotti 8, T 06 679 0405, www.gucci.com/it*

Babuino Novecento

Stefano Stagetti's tiny gem of a shop hosts exhibitions of original midcentury glass, ceramics and furniture. Expect to find rare pieces, such as this wood-framed 1952 armchair by Gio Ponti (above) that we spied on one visit. Other recommended stores are Maurizio de Nisi (T 06 474 0732), which sells furnishings from the 1930s and 1940s, and Retrò (T 06 6819 2746), a treasure trove of 20th-century design. For more contemporary pieces, head to the three-floor Spazio Sette (T 06 686 9747), which sells Cassina, Capellini, Kartell, Knoll and Zanotta, among others, and Magazzini Associati (T 06 6813 5179), a primary distributor of DePadova.
Via del Babuino 65, T 06 3600 3853, www.babuinonovecento.com

R-01-IOS
The flagship store of Paolo Giacomelli
and Roberta Paolucci's jewellery brand
Iosselliani, which launched in Rome in
1997, was converted from a 1950s bar, and
features the original kaleidoscopic tiles.
The dark walls provide a dramatic backdrop
for Iosselliani's snake-shaped rings, 1980s-
inspired necklaces and sleek earrings.
Via del Pigneto 39, T 06 7061 3527,
www.iosselliani.com

Bocca di Dama

Named after a delicious almond cake, Bocca di Dama in San Lorenzo is a patisserie with a serious design slant that revisits traditional recipes. Stock up on chocolate biscuits in natty packaging, multicoloured fruit tarts and pistachio cakes. The patisserie serves breakfasts, brunches, coffee and tea in intimate but fashionable surroundings, as well as offering catering services. If, after your sugar fix, you fancy a moment of literary reflection, visit nearby Bar à Book (Via dei Piceni 23, T 06 45445438), a popular little venue in the area that combines the joys of reading with a good wine list and retro interiors by Michele Peretto.
Via dei Marsi 2, T 06 4434 1154,
www.boccadidama.it

Nia

In a city so reluctant to adopt innovative retail architecture, the recent refit by fashionable Roman architectural practice Morq makes Nia a pleasant surprise. Situated in one of the prettiest shopping streets behind main strip Via del Corso, Nia boasts long white corridors, high vaulted ceilings and clever revolving shelving units. Ladies who lunch frequent this boutique crammed full with canvas beach bags, shoes and comfy neutral linen trousers. Labels on sale are mostly Nia's own brand, a mix of ethnic and dressy, but there are also a few safe French bets such as Vanessa Bruno and Antik Batik. There is a pretty patio terrace at the back where you can relax after your shopping spree.
Via Vittoria 48, T 06 679 5198,
www.niaroma.it

Roscioli

This jam-packed shop/restaurant/wine bar was opened in 2002 by Pierluigi and Alessandro Roscioli, who come from a family of well-known Roman bakers – their father runs the nearby Antico Forno Roscioli (T 06 686 4045). The cheese and ham counter here boasts the best of Italy's regional produce, while the selection of Italian and French wines is extensive. If you want to linger, stay for lunch and order Roscioli's signature *pasta alla carbonara*, fresh fish from Anzio and Civitavecchia, or slow-baked pizza – just make sure you've booked ahead. Foodies also flock to Volpetti (T 06 574 2352) in Testaccio; its Pecorino Fosse Venturi cheese, seasoned in caves for three months, is delicious with some fig jam. *Via dei Giubbonari 21, T 06 687 5287, www.anticofornoroscioli.com*

Secondo me
Snap up upcoming Italian talents at design gallery Secondo me. The collaboration between Benetton's communication group and Claudia Pignatale has rapidly grown into a success story, which led to this new outpost in 2010. The gallery has recently launched Cut & Paste, a seven-piece collection by designer Kiki van Eijk. *Via degli Orsini 26, www.secondome.eu*

B-Gallery

Tucked away in one of Rome's prettiest and lesser-known squares, home to the Basilica of Santa Cecilia, B-Gallery is a welcome respite from the bustle of Trastevere's crowded streets. Inside the two-floor bookshop/café/exhibition space, browse through the architecture, design, lifestyle and photography books, in both Italian and English, and then drop down to the lower level, to see multimedia installations and exhibitions by international and Italian artists, as well as the odd dancing event. Sunday brunch here is a relaxed and convivial affair, with salads, cappuccinos and juices served by friendly staff with a great taste in music. In the evening at *aperitivo* hour, a wide selection of wines is served. *Piazza Santa Cecilia 16, T 06 5833 4365, www.b-gallery.it*

Nora P

Eleonora Pastore is the former owner of one of the most fashionable florists in Rome, so it's hardly a surprise to learn that her new adventure, Nora P, is another success. The concept of the shop is that of an outdoor/indoor emporium that sells vintage and modern furniture, garden furniture, jewellery, houseware, 1950s ceramics and the amusing Mook sculptures. On display are also works by assorted Italian artists such as Giorgia Galanti, Claudio Romei and Elizabeth Frolei. Do keep an eye out for an eclectic assembly of chairs, tables and plants, as well as the little patio terrace at the back. *Via Panisperna 220-221, T 06 4547 3738, www.nora-p.com*

SPORTS AND SPAS

WORK OUT, CHILL OUT OR JUST WATCH

A decent workout will get you in shape for the cultural assault course that constitutes Rome's myriad sites. Located in the city's embassy district, Dabliù Parioli (Viale Romania 22, T 06 807 5577) has Technogym machines, an aqua gym, a beauty salon and a Thermarium spa zone with a sauna, Turkish bath and hydro-massage; a first-timer's day pass costs €20. The Roman Sport Center (Viale del Galoppatoio 33, T 06 320 1667) in Villa Borghese park has a similar range of facilities; day passes here cost €30. The triathlon champion Danilo Palmucci is one of Rome's top personal trainers, and works from the Fitnext Sports Centre (Piazza Mignanelli 23, T 06 679 6003). Our pick of the best day spas includes Kami Spa (opposite) that specialises in oriental therapy; the futuristic, unisex Acanto Benessere Spa (see p093); the gorgeous hammam Acqua Madre (Via di Sant' Ambrogio 17, T 06 686 4272); and recently opened Equilibrio (via Giolitti 34, t 06 97 60 6184), highly recommended for couples' treatments.

As sweltering temperatures are the norm in Rome between April and November, an escape from the city is often essential. Head for the beach in Fregene or Castel Porziano, or further south to Torre Paola, near Sabaudia (see p098). The equestrian school I Due Laghi (Via della Marmotta, T 06 9960 7059) in Anguillara Sabazia on Lake Bracciano is one of Italy's best, and offers diving and golfing. *For full addresses, see Resources.*

Kami Spa

Escape the hustle and bustle of Piazza di Spagna by stepping into Kami's rarified, zen-like atmosphere. This Italian-owned spa is a temple to the oriental art of wellbeing. Its five floors and 20 staff members are devoted to Chinese, Indonesian, Japanese, Thai and Indian treatments. The décor has a geographic theme for each room, the Chinese room featuring four-poster beds and the Japanese one tatami mats and screens. On the menu are hot stone therapy, Bali coffee scrub, traditional Thai massage, Balinese palm massage and the Oriental blend – a mix of Thai, shiatsu and lomi massages. Once you're done, you can relax with a cup of green tea in the sitting room, gazing at the pretty patio .
Via degli Avignonesi 12, T 06 4200 3624
www.kamispa.com

Wonderfool
Stressed-out aristocrats, actors and
execs have been flocking to this men's
spa since it was launched by former
advertising manager Prospero Di Veroli
in 2007. Kitted out with art deco-
inspired furnishings, the interior has
a clubby feel and includes a Turkish
bath, treatment rooms and fitness area.
*Via dei Banchi Nuovi 39, T 06 6889 2315,
www.wonderfool.it*

Stadio Olimpico

This football ground, completed in 1937 and modernised for the 1990 World Cup, hosts matches for the city's two Serie A teams, Roma and Lazio, almost every Sunday from September until late May. If you like your games to be fuelled by the enthusiasm of local supporters, buy the cheaper tickets in the *curva* section of the stadium – just remember that the *Romanisti* are in the *curva sud* (the cheapest tickets cost around €15), while the *Laziali* are to be found in the *curva nord* (also from about €15). For a more civilised experience, and a guaranteed numbered seat, splash out on tickets in the *tribuna numerata* (which start at €33). Tickets can be bought from the clubs' websites, or at one of the many Roma or Lazio stores in the city centre.
Via dei Discoboli, T 06 36 851

Acanto Benessere Spa

Located in Centro Storico, the unisex Acanto spa offers treatments that replicate the beautifying rituals of the ancient Romans. Although many are geared towards hydrotherapy, you can also be plucked, preened and pummelled in the ethereal glass treatment rooms, which form part of the spa's futuristic interior, created by architects Marco and Gianluigi Giammetta. After you've finished, wander into the adjoining Caffè Universale (T 06 6839 2065) to browse in the bookshop; buy condiments in the deli; settle down with a coffee in the café; or reverse the benefits of your treatment in the smoking room.
Piazza Rondanini 30, T 06 6813 6602, www.acantospa.it

Palazzo delle Terme

Opened in 1937, these baths, along with the Stadio dei Marmi (see p037) and Stadio Olimpico (see p092), form part of northern Rome's Foro Italico. Previously known as Foro Mussolini, the sports complex was commissioned by Il Duce. Although what was the dictator's private gym at Palazzo delle Terme is off limits to the public, the Olympic-size pool is open to all. The main attractions aren't the sight of the sexy locals splashing about, the opportunity to cool down or enjoy an invigorating workout, it's the chance to see the mosaics of muscular swimmers, boxers and wrestlers that adorn the high walls, and striking but alarming Fascist slogans, which grace the tiled floors.
Piazza Lauro De Bosis 3, T 06 3685 7564

ESCAPES

WHERE TO GO IF YOU WANT TO LEAVE TOWN

The ancient wonders and Renaissance masterpieces at Rome's core seem all the more magical when compared to the hideous suburban sprawl that surrounds it. When you're planning a day trip and thinking of renting a car, make sure your chosen driver is brave enough to tackle the Roman traffic. For an out-of-town picnic amid spectacular surroundings, head for Tivoli and the formal gardens of the 16th-century Villa d'Este palace (Piazza Trento 1, T 07 7433 2920) and the ruins of Emperor Hadrian's retreat, Villa Adriana (Via di Villa Adriana 204, T 06 3996 7900). Meanwhile, for oenophiles, a tour of the vineyards of Frascati is a good choice, whereas beach-lovers should take the hydrofoil from Anzio to the island of Ponza (opposite).

When the heat in town is truly unbearable, head for Lake Bracciano to take a dip before lunch at Vino e Camino (Piazza Mazzini 11, T 06 9980 3433) in the main square, under the shade of the stunning Orsini castle. The perfect antidote to post-flight fatigue is to book yourself in to John Paul Getty's luxurious former getaway, La Posta Vecchia (Palo Laziale, Ladispoli, T 06 994 9501), with its sweeping seascapes and elegant landscaped gardens. Alternatively, stay overnight at Il Pellicano (Località Sbarcatello, Porto Ercole, T 05 6485 8111) in Tuscany, for some great local cuisine and restorative sun-worshipping.

For full addresses, see Resources.

Ponza

A 70-minute hydrofoil journey from nearby Anzio will take you to Ponza, a tiny, rugged island. A favourite playground of wealthy Romans, it fills up fast at peak times, so it's best to visit slightly out of season. Sun-lovers and revellers swear by Il Frontone, the only sandy beach on the island, which is accessible by boat from the port. From sunset onwards, order a cocktail from the beach bar and join in the dancing. For superb fish, try Orèstorante (T 07 718 0338) or Acqua Pazza (T 07 718 0643) on the seafront. Set above the port, it's hardly surprising that the Fendi family's *pensione*, Villa Laetitia Ponza (T 07 7180 9886), is among the most stylish on the island; one of its best rooms is the Zafferano (above).

Sabaudia

If you've been seduced by Mussolini's monumental Fascist developments EUR (see p068) and the Foro Italico, visit the seaside resort of Sabaudia, Il Duce's most impressive example of rationalist town planning, where tree-lined avenues are linked by towers painted in 'Sabaudia yellow'. Don't miss the post office (overleaf), an orgy of blue *tesserae*, or the Chiesa SS Annunziata (right). Il Complesso Punta Rossa (T 07 7354 8085), a short drive away, is a swish place to spend the night. Back in Rome, Garbatella, the housing project he created for the blue-collar workers whose original homes he bulldozed, is also worth a tour. Take a turn round Piazza Bartolomeo Romano and Piazza Benedetto Brin, and then dine on fennel and blood-orange salad, and polenta with veal rolls at Al Ristoro degli Angeli (T 06 5143 6020).

Post office, Sabaudia

Villa Metato, Umbria
Siena and Montone are both in striking
distance of Villa Metato, a perfect
one-bedroom Umbrian bolt-hole. Set
in 12 acres of gardens, its 18th-century
façade belies its modern interior, which
was created by photographer Nick
Ferrand and his wife, stylist Margherita
Gardella. You won't want to leave.
Morra, Città di Castello, T 07 5857 4115,
www.villametato.com

NOTES

SKETCHES AND MEMOS

RESOURCES
CITY GUIDE DIRECTORY

HOTELS

ADDRESSES AND ROOM RATES

Aleph 020
Room rates:
double, €235;
Deluxe Room, €280;
Junior Suite, €585
Via di San Basilio 15
T 06 422 901
www.aleph.boscolohotels.com

Anahi 023
Room rates:
double, from €110
Via della Penna 65
T 06 361 0841
www.hotelanahi.com

Casa Manni 022
Room rates:
double, from €600
Via di Pietra 70
T 06 9727 4787
www.casamanni.com

Hotel Capo d'Africa 016
Room rates:
double, €380
Via Capo d'Africa 54
T 06 772 801
www.hotelcapodafrica.com

Il Complessa Punta Rossa 098
Room rates:
double, from €200
Via delle Batterie 37
San Felice Circeo
T 07 7354 8085

Hotel Eden 016
Room rates:
double, €365
Via Ludovisi 49
T 06 478 121
www.hotel-eden.it

Fortyseven 016
Room rates:
double, from €180
Via Luigi Petroselli 47
T 06 678 7816
www.fortysevenhotel.com

Hotel Hassler 016
Room rates:
double, from €385
Piazza della Trinità dei Monti 6
T 06 699 340
www.hotelhasslerroma.com

Leon's Place 017
Room rates:
double, from €270;
Junior Suite, €400
Via 20 Settembre 90/94
T 06 890 871

Hotel Locarno 023
Room rates:
double, from €180;
Rooms 602 and 605, from €400;
Venetian Suite, from €500
Via della Penna 22
T 06 361 0841
www.hotellocarno.com .

Il Palazzetto 021
Room rates:
double, from €275;
Room 2, from €275
Vicolo del Bottino 8
T 06 699 341 000
www.ilpalazzettoroma.com

Il Pellicano 096
Room rates:
double, from €440
Località Sbarcatello
Porto Ercole
Tuscany
T 05 6485 8111
www.pellicanohotel.com

Portrait Suites 024
Room rates:
Studio, from €390;
Suite, from €570;
Penthouse, from €1,650
Via Bocca di Leone 23
T 06 6938 0742
www.rome-suites-portrait.com

La Posta Vecchia 030
Room rates:
double, from €350
Palo Laziale
Ladispoli
T 06 994 9501
www.lapostavecchia.com

Raphael Hotel 016
Room rates:
double, from €190
Largo Febo 2
T 06 682 831
www.raphaelhotel.com

Hotel de Russie 026
Room rates:
double, €680;
Deluxe Room, €840;
Popolo Suite, €2,800
Via del Babuino 9
T 06 328 881
www.hotelderussie.it

St George 028
Room rates:
double, from €280;
Deluxe Room, from €340;
Junior Suite, from €430
Via Giulia 62
T 06 686 611
www.stgeorgehotel.it

Villa Laetitia 028
Room rates:
double, €190;
Karl Room, €350;
Atelier Suite, €350
Lungotevere delle Armi 22-23
T 06 322 6776
www.villalaetitia.com

Villa Laetitia Ponza 097
Room rates:
double, from €105;
Zafferano, from €105
Salita Scotti
Ponza
Isole Pontine
T 07 7180 9886
www.villalaetitia.com

Villa Metato 102
Room rates:
Villa, from €250
Morra
Città di Castello
Umbria
T 07 5857 4115
www.villametato.com

WALLPAPER* CITY GUIDES

Editorial Director
Richard Cook

Art Director
Loran Stosskopf
Editor
Rachael Moloney
O'ar Pali
Authors
Giovanna Dunmall
Sara Manuelli
Deputy Editor
Jeremy Case

Senior Designer
Eriko Shimazaki
Designer
Lara Collins

Map Illustrator
Russell Bell

Photography Editor
Sophie Corben
Photography Assistant
Robin Key

Sub-Editors
Stephen Patience
Rachel Ward
Editorial Assistant
Ella Marshall

**Wallpaper* Group
Editor-in-Chief**
Tony Chambers
Publishing Director
Gord Ray

Contributors
Emma Blau
Sara Henrichs
Meirion Pritchard

Wallpaper* ® is a
registered trademark
of IPC Media Limited

First published 2006
Second edition 2008
Third edition (revised
and updated) 2009
Fourth edition (revised
and updated) 2010
© 2006, 2008, 2009
and 2010
IPC Media Limited

ISBN 978 0 7148 6090 9

PHAIDON

Phaidon Press Limited
Regent's Wharf
All Saints Street
London N1 9PA

Phaidon Press Inc
180 Varick Street
New York, NY 10014

Phaidon® is a registered
trademark of Phaidon
Press Limited

www.phaidon.com

All prices are correct at
time of going to press,
but are subject to change.

Printed in China

PHOTOGRAPHERS

Iwan Baan
Maxxi, p,065, pp066-067

Jeroen Bergmans
St Peter's Basilica, p015
Piazza Navona, pp034-035

Bjørn A. Jørgensen
Accademia di Danimarca,
p069

Oliviero Olivieri
Rome city view,
inside front cover
Pantheon, p010
Termini station, p011
Colosseum, pp012-013
Aventine post office, p014
Aleph, p020
Il Palazzetto, p021
Hotel Locarno, p023
Villa Laetitia, pp028-029
Cul de Sac, p036
Stadio dei Marmi, p037
Bar Necci, p046
Primo, p059
La Casa del Caffè Tazza
d'Oro, pp056-057
Il Baretto, p058
Palazzo della Civiltà del
Lavoro, p068
Auditorium Parco della
Musica, pp070-071
Stadio Olimpico, p092
Palazzo delle Terme,
pp094-095

Ming Tang Evans
Portrait Suites, pp024-025
Casa Manni, p022
Hotel de Russie, p027
St George, pp030-031
MACRO, p033
Urbana 47, p041,
pp042-043
Caffè della Pace, p045
Salotto Locarno, p047
Tree Bar, p048
Ristorante Angelina,
p049, pp050-051
Pastificio San Lorenzo,
pp052-053
Obikà, p054
SAID Chocolate Factory,
p055
Tati al 28, pp060-061
Livia Risi, p063
Super, p073
Motelsalieri, pp074-075
R-01-IOS, pp078-079
Bacco di Dama,
p080, p081
Nia, p082
Roscioli, p083
Secondome, pp084-085
B-Gallery, pp086
Nora P, p087
Kami Spa, p089

Tommaso Sartori
Chiesa SS Annunziata,
Sabaudia, pp098-099
Post office, Sabaudia,
pp100-101

ROME

A COLOUR-CODED GUIDE TO THE CITY'S HOT 'HOODS

CENTRO STORICO
The domed Pantheon and Piazza Navona bookend an area tantalisingly rich in history

PIGNETO
Hedonists make for this former working-class area, now home to loft-dwelling creatives

ANCIENT ROME
It may take imagination to visualise how the Forum once looked, but not the Colosseum

MONTI AND ESQUILINO
In Rome, even the former slums have style. Esquilino is one of the city's hot 'hoods

TRASTEVERE
The bohos have long been priced out by expat bankers, but the nightlife is still kicking

TRIDENTE
In the madness that is a Roman summer, the Villa Borghese park is an urban oasis

TESTACCIO
This ancient rubbish dump now boasts fashionable nightclubs and hip bars aplenty

VIA VENETO
La Dolce Vita was shot here, but only recently has the area been getting its groove back

For a full description of each neighbourhood, see the Introduction.
Featured venues are colour-coded, according to the district in which they are located.